MASTER YOUR
WOW

MASTER YOUR
WOW

DISCOVER THE REAL
SECRET OF THE RICH

VISHAL MORJARIA

WOW Book Publishing™

First edition published by WOW Book Publishing™ and
Vishal Morjaria at WowBookPublishing.com

www.MasterYourWow.com

Copyright © 2018 Vishal Morjaria

ISBN: 978-1976212789

Warning—Disclaimer

Dedication

I wrote this book so that you can discover that you not only have a book inside you, but that it's also possible to get it done super fast—within only three days.

    I dedicate this book to the wonder and splendour within you in the hope that the words and message inspire you to do something special and great with your life.

Love,

—Vishal Morjaria
International Speaker and Award-Winning Author

Table of Contents

Testimonials for
Master Your WOW

"Books are very important; I would actually have written books sooner, and Vishal teaches you how to write the right book and get it out in the world within 3 days. This book will serve you well on your journey."

—**Jack Canfield, Star of the hit movie**
***The Secret*, Co-creator of**
the *Chicken Soup for the Soul* series,
and Leading Transformational Coach
and Speaker

"This book contains a genuine secret that all wealthy people know, and Vishal truly wants you to know it and apply it, too. Use it wisely, for it will take your business and income to the next level."

—**Loral Langemeier,**
Star of hit movie *The Secret* and
New York Times Bestselling Author

"With his knowledge, Vishal is the definition of an exponential leader in the personal and professional development sector. His latest book *Master Your WOW* will guarantee your brand reaches the next level of world class if you follow his masterfully developed step-by-step strategies."

—**Arun Nadarasa, UK**
Author of *Pharmacy Movement—How to Prescribe*
Social and Digital Medicines

"If you want to know anything about marketing, sales, speaking, and entrepreneurship in general, you definitely need to check out Vishal. I've been in business for nearly 30 years, and Vishal could still teach me things I've never heard of before. Besides all that, he is such a generous person to be with. He will not rest until his clients are happy."

—Tineke Rensen, Holland
CEO of Powerful Business Academy and
Author of *Maximum Business Growth for Women*

"Vishal helped me realise my dream of writing my first book, and now I'm already on my second one! I'm happy to be able to connect with the rest of the world through my words. Vishal has empowered me with such great energy and motivation, and I hope I can do the same for others soon."

—Marie Varlin, Guadeloupe, Caribbean
Author of *Le Secret du Bien Être*,
TV Presenter and Producer

'Vishal's latest book *Master Your WOW* is fantastic! It's easy to read yet thought-provoking. His book takes you through a transformational journey that will give you the confidence to take your business to the next level. Thank you, Vishal for sharing and inspiring us to be better."

—Diahann Holder, USA
Di-Namic Consulting, Financial Coach,
and Author of *Financial Freedom for Women*

"Vishal delivered an outstanding experience at the WOW Book Camp™! The techniques he will teach you in order to start and complete your book in three days are amazing and mind-blowing. It will never again be a terrifying task."

—**Teo Palmieri, USA**
Real Estate Broker at Elite Ocean View Realty,
Author of the upcoming book
Keep it Real in Real Estate

"Vishal has a true gift to enable ordinary people to live extraordinary lives. Before meeting Vishal I didn't believe that is was possible for me to achieve great things, but now he has shown me a path to exceptional branding and becoming a great author. Vishal is an incredible professional speaker and an inspiration to us all. His latest book *Master Your WOW* will take you to new heights in order to reach your personal and financial goals, so watch and listen very carefully. Absolute WOW!"

—**CJ Xander, UK**
Founder of Discouragement into Recognition

"Vishal and his latest book *Master Your WOW* really help you brand yourself and get your business out into the world. It has been eye-opening and has positively changed my perception of branding."

—**Dr Lalitaa Suglani, UK**
CEO of The Personal Success Academy and
Author of *Your Mirror Mirror*

"*Master Your Wow* is written by a true master entrepreneur, speaker, and sales coach—Vishal Morjaria. Vishal is a powerful teacher who has a gift to really transform your business and your life. My personal branding journey began after attending Vishal's WOW Book Camp™, and in a very short period of time I saw my business and finances improve quite dramatically. If you have a message that you want to bring to the world and you want to get that message out FAST, then Vishal's teachings are a must!"

—Hiten Bhatt, Leadership Trainer & Coach, UK
Director of BE GREAT Training, UK
Author of *The Leadership Adventure*

"*Master your WOW* will transform your life and open your eyes to taking your expertise and knowledge to a new level. Vishal delivers his content in a simple and very doable manner, suited to all ages and abilities. You will learn the true secrets to growing your business, understanding what it takes to be successful and how you can write a book regardless of your background or perceived ability—yes, written and completed in just 3 days! Vishal is passionate about helping those who truly want to succeed, and he will help you find 'your' voice. Enjoy the journey and future that lies ahead."

—Juliet Robinson aka Sanity Nanny, UK
Child Sleep & Family Lifestyle Coach and
Author of *Wits' End to Wise Parent*

About the Author

Vishal wrote this book so that you can write yours.

The award-winning author currently lives in the UK but travels extensively across the world conducting seminars and workshops to help ordinary people discover their extraordinary potential and transform their professional and personal lives.

Vishal transformed his life by turning the difficult experiences he had into positive life lessons. From struggling hard to make ends meet and suffering from clinical depression, Vishal transformed himself into an award-winning author and a highly successful transformational coach and speaker.

Vishal believes that you have the right to lead a life that fulfils your potential, and this is evident in the diverse lifestyles of the people he has inspired. The people who attend his workshops include aspiring entrepreneurs as well as disillusioned and dissatisfied professionals who want to see better results for their efforts.

Learn more about Vishal at www.MasterYourWow.com

Foreword

Dear Reader,

*Master Your WOW is **the** book you need to read and learn about in order to get and stay recognised as an authority in your industry and profession.*

Vishal has acquired some masterful skills and knowledge, and he imparts it to you in a way that will allow you to understand and apply it immediately.

The knowledge in this book has the power to help you create the life that you truly deserve and desire. I can tell you that even being as successful as I am, I wish I had written books sooner, and Vishal will teach you to write your book within three days.

I can tell you from my 40+ years of experience in this industry that Vishal has the expertise, skills, spirit, and heart necessary to help you get your book out into the world in the right and most powerful way.

—Jack Canfield
Star of the hit movie *The Secret*
Co-creator of the *Chicken Soup for the Soul* series
Co-author of *The Success Principles*
Leading Transformational Coach and Speaker

Acknowledgements

I acknowledge the souls that are no longer here such as Mahatma Gandhi, Mother Theresa, Martin Luther King, Nelson Mandela, and Steve Jobs for having such a positive impact on humanity.

I'm grateful for the leadership of her Majesty The Queen, Barack Obama, Theresa May, Jeremy Corbyn, Former President Bill Clinton, Al Gore, Oprah Winfrey, Narendra Modi, and many others whom I've not named but who continue to tirelessly help make the world a better place for you and me.

I acknowledge the Brahma Kumaris World Spiritual University for the spiritual work they are doing in uplifting humanity.

I acknowledge some of the great business minds that I've had the pleasure of learning from and also being associated with, such as Warren Buffet, Sir Richard Branson, Jim Rohn, Zig Ziglar, Og Mandino, Robert Kiyosaki, Tony Robbins, Les Brown, and stars of the movie *The Secret* Bob Proctor, Jack Canfield, Dr John Gray, Lisa Nichols, Dr John Demartini, Loral Langemeier, Marie Diamond, and Levi Roots.

I acknowledge my family, friends, my staff, and supporters of this book for their help in the process of writing and creating it.

I acknowledge the divine energy and higher powers that be for assisting me in my journey with this book and my life.

Finally, I acknowledge you for receiving this book and using it in the most positive way that you know.

Note to the Reader

The information, including opinions and analyses, contained herein is based on the author's personal experiences and is not intended to provide professional advice.

The author and the publisher make no warranties, either expressed or implied, concerning the accuracy, applicability, effectiveness, reliability, or suitability of the contents. If you wish to apply or follow the advice or recommendations mentioned herein, you take full responsibility for your actions. The author and publisher of this book shall in no event be held liable for any direct, indirect, incidental, or consequential damages arising directly or indirectly from the use of any of the information contained in this book.

All content is for information only and is not warranted for content accuracy or any other implied or explicit purpose.

CHAPTER 1
Branding YOU

Branding YOU

The person who follows the crowd will usually go no further than the crowd. The person who walks alone is likely to find himself in places no one has ever seen before.

—*Albert Einstein*

D o you see other people when you look at yourself? You are the most important person in your life. Do you agree with this view? If you have any doubts, go and take a good, long look at yourself in the mirror. What do you see? Did you see John Lennon? Richard Branson? David Beckham? Did you see Paris Hilton? Oprah? No, you didn't see any of these people, did you?

Hold that thought right there! When I asked you if you see someone else, you assumed it was just a rhetorical question.

Now, really, put down this book, get up, and go look in the mirror. Yes, I know you did not do it the first time.

Let's face it—what you see is a reflection of yourself. But are you who you think you are? Are you who other people think you are? Do you know what others think about you or how they see you?

There is only one way to find out. Ask yourself these three questions:

Who are you?

What do you have to offer?

Why should anyone care?

I will go first.

I am Vishal Morjaria. I am the award-winning author of *Flab to FAB 'The Holistic Guide to Effortless Weight Loss.'* I am also the author of the book you are currently reading. I am who I am because I wrote these books on a professional level. I wrote these books because I recognised and realised that I had knowledge that I wanted to share with you so that you could benefit from reading my books.

Now, it is your turn.

What is your response? You can say, "I am (your name here) John Smith. I am 'a' _____" (your profession here— an accountant or a property developer or a businessperson or an entrepreneur). "I am who I am because _____." If you are an accountant, you may say something like, "I am an accountant because I am good with numbers," or "I am a businessperson because I like to make money." But how does this distinguish you from other accountants or businesspeople?

You need to go from being 'an' ordinary person to 'the' special or extraordinary person to create an impression. Otherwise, you are just another individual who's in the basket of boring, just like the rest of them. I am not trying to be rude, but it's the truth. No one cares if you're perceived to be exactly the same as all the others, but if you can stand out, be bold, and are different, at the worst you'll get noticed. That is an achievement in itself, because most people go through life unnoticed.

You see me as the authority on a particular subject because I wrote the book about it. Whereas, despite all the knowledge and wisdom you may have accumulated over the years, other people may, at best, perceive you as an expert. That is what other people see. The truth is that *most* experts are pretty broke, but almost all authorities are wealthy. Why? Experts themselves recognise that they are knowledgeable, but authorities are recognised as knowledgeable by *other people,* too. These people are the ones that will see value in your knowledge and pay you so you can get wealthy or rich.

Do you see the difference between being an expert and being an authority?

If you had asked me to answer these three questions a few years back, my answers would have been quite similar to yours. The point is that there are a million or more people like you. You are not seeing a reflection of yourself in the mirror because the most important person now in your life is not you; it is the people around you.

Your reflection is the same as their reflection. You are not seeing someone special. You are seeing someone ordinary. The same as everyone else.

You are stuck in the same traffic jams, you stand in the same queues, you do the same thing, day after day, and at the end of the month you struggle to make ends meet. It is the same story all over again the next month, and the next year, and before you realise, it is too late to do anything about it.

At the moment, you see someone who is just like everyone

else. You are not seeing a reflection of yourself. You are seeing a reflection of everyone else.

Get Out of the Basket of Boring

You are in the basket of boring. You may think that you are satisfied and content in the basket of boring, but it's an illusion. This illusion is created by your own delusion that this is all you can be. You may be under the false impression that the basket of boring is a comfortable place to be. It is not. You are slowly but surely diminishing your own individuality. You are merging with the background.

The truth is, you are actually falling further towards the bottom of the basket.

But this should not be you, because you are, in fact, unique.

Look at successful people. What separates successful people from the rest?

Successful people are noticed. You do not see through them. They attract attention and, in turn, attract opportunities, people, and wealth.

Success may mean many things to different people. However, what most of us would agree is that successful people do not just have material wealth; they are also happy and popular. In other words, they may have reached an extraordinary state of emotional, social, and perhaps even spiritual balance.

They rarely get upset when things do not go as expected. They feel at home whether they are alone or in the company of friends, colleagues, or acquaintances. They have found a place in the hearts and minds of people around them.

So, how do successful people achieve this state? They do so by attracting opportunities to utilise their talent and skills, connecting with other people and generating appreciation, goodwill, and sometimes even praise for their efforts, which converts to a reliable means of income.

Successful people rise above the ordinary. They escape the basket of boring and establish their presence on the Island of Individuality.

If you want to be successful, you should attract more attention and more opportunities, which in turn will attract more clients and a higher income.

Therefore, the first step to Master Your WOW is to create your own signature. How do you do this? By Branding YOU as an individual, unique and distinct from everyone else.

The Four Most Powerful Ways of Branding

When you buy something, you are buying either a product or the brand. You can buy an MP3 player. Alternatively, you can buy '*the* iPod'. Similarly, you can buy a car or you can buy '*the* ultimate driving machine.'

You could go on holiday to a beach resort, similar to the one you went to last year, or the year before that. Alternatively, you could go to someplace extraordinary. You could climb Mt Fuji or Mt Kilimanjaro, go scuba diving in the Maldives, or witness the great Serengeti Wildebeest migration.

You can do what others are doing, or you can do what few have done, or even what no one else has done.

Whether you are a plumber or a pianist, an executive or an entrepreneur, you need to create an aura of noticeability around you. You need to come out of the basket of boring and establish your own Island of Individuality.

No amount of talent or hard work can match a deliberate and systematic approach to making your presence felt. You are an individual, and if you want others to look at you in the same way, then you need to turn the spotlight on you.

You may be under the impression that modesty is a virtue and that bragging about yourself is not an attractive quality. This does not, however, mean that you should merge into the crowd. You need to assert your individuality and raise the flag of your potential to perform. Only then will you gain opportunities to prove your capabilities.

Look at successful people around you. They are noticed. People trust them because they know they can deliver. Successful people are visible, and they are credible.

If you want to become successful, you also need to acquire the qualities of being Known and Respected. How do you do this?

By branding YOU as an individual. By turning yourself from someone unknown and unnoticeable to a branded personality, an individual who stands out, one who just cannot be ignored—and when people meet you once, they will remember you forever.

So, in what ways can you achieve this?

There are four simple yet powerful ways of establishing your personal brand. In the same way a product is developed into a brand that stands apart from other 'me-too' commodity products, you can also transform yourself into a brand. When you have your own personal brand, you will attract attention and opportunities to generate more income and wealth.

The Quadruple A Branding Battery

You may have heard of the battery that goes on and on. Do you realise that I do not even have to mention the brand name of the battery? Even without mentioning it, you already know which brand of battery I am talking about. This is exactly what the Quadruple A (or the AAAA) Branding Battery can do for you.

It can transform you from being anonymous to being recognised, and even to being the subject of discussion and debate when you are not physically present.

So, here are the four powerful ways of branding yourself.

1. Branding by Association
2. Branding by Acknowledgement
3. Branding by Achievement
4. Branding by Authoring

Branding by Association

Branding by Association is the first step to establishing your individuality. When you associate yourself with well-known personalities, their credibility and visibility enhances your own personal brand. There are many ways you can achieve this: through networking, attending seminars and conferences, or taking part in collaborative projects.

Let us say you are a Chartered Accountant and you know Robert Kiyosaki, the author of the "Rich Dad Poor

Dad" books. Since you know Robert Kiyosaki, and have met him, you might be in possession of a picture of the two of you hanging out together. Consider the impact that you could have by uploading this picture on your website, social networking profile, or even using it as part of a presentation.

When people associate you with a famous personality, they think that you are someone important. You immediately develop an aura of impact and influence. It is in many ways similar to the effect of turning on a spotlight. People start noticing you because you are no longer in the shadows. You are no longer falling deeper into the basket of boring.

However, it is not easy nor is it always possible for you to have the opportunity to associate with someone who is well known. However, despair not, for there are other ways to brand YOU. That is why it is called the Quadruple A Branding Battery. There are three more ways you can become Known and Respected.

Branding by Acknowledgement

Branding by Acknowledgement means asking people to express their opinion about you. It is not unlike a brand, book, or movie to get positive reviews from trusted critics. When people hear about you from a third person, it creates better credibility than simply blowing your own trumpet ever could.

Let us say you are a property consultant. When you say you are good at what you do, why should people believe you? Now, consider this. Have you helped some of the eminent and respected personalities in your city or town to find their dream houses? Have you helped well-known companies relocate their offices to a more prominent and better equipped business district? Can these former clients attest to that?

Imagine the mayor of your city stating on your business card, brochure, or website, "John is my favourite property consultant." You will immediately be perceived as a very important and accomplished property consultant, because you have a testimonial from none other than the Mayor, vouching for your expertise and ability to deliver results.

Do you see how being Known and Respected can give you Branding by Acknowledgement? Now, it is not always very easy to get acknowledgements or testimonials from people who matter. This is especially the case if you are young and just starting your career.

Let us take a look at the third A in the Quadruple A Branding Battery.

Branding by Achievement

If you want people to take notice of you, then you have to demonstrate that you are better than average. To do so, you have to rise above mediocrity and prove that you are the cream on the top, not just another me-too face in the crowd. You have to establish your superior credentials in any profession or industry.

Branding by Achievement is about announcing the milestones, awards, and accolades that you have received. Even a small recognition bestows credibility on you in the eyes of potential clients or customers—do not ignore any achievement, however small. Leverage your achievements to strengthen your personal brand.

For instance, a hitherto obscure movie suddenly shoots into the news and into people's consciousness when it wins an award at a Film Festival. The Film Festival need not be an international event for the movie to gain recognition; it can even be a regional affair. Similarly, copies of a book that have been gathering dust on the display shelves in bookstores suddenly start disappearing as readers vie to lay their hands on it when the writer is interviewed on radio or TV. It need not be someone as well known as Oprah (that would be the ultimate compliment), but even an interview on the local radio show can sometimes do the trick.

So, how do you gain these kinds of achievements for your brand? By taking part in industry-related activities. However, as you know, when it comes to industry-related recognitions or awards, there are only one, two or, at the most, three winners. So, what do you do?

Your achievements need not always be about coming first; they can also be about trying. Imagine for a moment you are a physical trainer. If you simply *take part* in a marathon, even that can be portrayed and perceived as an achievement.

Of course, if you came first in the marathon—that is great! But even if you only just finished running the 26.2-mile distance—that is still an achievement. Start with small achievements and then build your brand with bigger and better awards and accolades.

What if you do not know anyone famous, and therefore Branding by Association is not possible? What if you do not have any testimonials, which means Branding by Acknowledgement is out of the question? What if achieving any level of recognition is not so easy in your professional area, and so Branding by Achievement is not an option?

The good news is, you still have another option. This is the fourth A in the Quadruple A Branding Battery.

Branding by Authoring

Branding by Authoring is by far the most underutilised and yet also the most doable option. When you introduce yourself to people or give them your business card, do people say, "Oh, well, thanks"?

Do you want them to instead say, "Wow"?

Try giving them a book instead of a business card. Not just any book. Give them a book that you wrote.

I have trouble writing my own CV, so how can I expect to write a book?

English isn't my first language, and wouldn't writing a book in English be way out of my league?

What can I write about? Why would anyone be interested in reading what I write?

Shouldn't I be working hard in my profession or my business, instead of writing a book?

What good can writing a book do? Will I make any money by writing a book?

I will leave a few blank lines for you to write any other excuses you can think of for not writing a book.

_____

_____

_____

_____

Now, if you have gone through all the excuses you can think of for not writing a book, let's look at how Branding by Authoring can catapult you from being an unknown, unnoticeable, nameless face in the crowd to someone who is visible and credible.

As Michael E. Gerber, known as "the World's No. 1 Small Business Guru," and author of the bestselling book *Awakening the Entrepreneur Within* and the *E-Myth* series of books, says, "Work on your business, not in your business."

If you had one day to work on your business, what would you do?

Would you go out and try to get new clients? Would you spend that time searching for courses to enrol in to attain a new educational or professional qualification? Would you spend it on writing a new CV? Would you spend it on writing a new slogan or tagline for your business?

Or would you write a book?

The idea of spending your precious time writing a book may sound surprising to you, but let me explain how it can transform your personal brand in ways you may not have imagined.

You Don't Sell Your Book—Your Book Sells You

Dr John Gray, author of *Men are from Mars, Women are from Venus*, once said, "I'd rather have a book than a PhD."

Dr Gray explained, "If you are an author, the media would want to interview you. They would prefer an author to a PhD." Similarly, if you want to be taken seriously, you need to be perceived as an authority and not just as an expert.

If you have written a book, you must be important. If you have written a book, you have created something of value. Therefore, you must be someone who matters.

Your book acts as a catalyst and automatically catapults you from anonymity to being perceived as an authority.

Do you know what it is that the wealthy have that others don't? It is, of course, being Known and Respected. When you hear of someone who is in the top of their profession or business, you can clearly see that they are better than the rest and that they are trustworthy.

If you want to make your way from the crowd to the top 1% who have made it big, who possess not only wealth but are also Known and Respected, then you have to command attention and be perceived as an authority.

When you write your book, you are automatically perceived as the authority in that subject area.

Imagine sending a book that you have written along with your CV instead of sending just a CV. Can they afford not to call you for an interview? They cannot. Whether it is a job interview or a media interview, the moment anyone sees that you have written a book, they perceive you as a giant source of wisdom, an authority, someone worth meeting and talking with.

Imagine yourself giving them a book instead of handing over a business card. Will that person ever forget you?

You have a book in you, and it is time to get it out.

Branding by WOW

When you see a rainbow in the sky, you hold your breath. Why? It is because a rainbow is a rare occurrence; not an everyday affair. Similarly, you should create the impression that you are a rarity. In any field, there are people who do the ordinary, and there are those who rise above.

How many people do you personally know or have you met who have written a book? Is it a few, one or two, or zero?

Nobody in my family has ever written a book before me. English is not even my first language. Despite all this, I wrote a book. So can you—if you know how. In this book, you will learn not just how to write a book, but also how to create a WOW and how to Master Your WOW.

When a prospective client or business partner hears that you have written a book, they cannot believe it. When you then give them a copy of your book, they are in awe. They say WOW!

They now recognise that you are not just someone ordinary but someone who is exceptional. When you write a book, you go from sitting idly in the basket of boring to someone who is an authority, someone who has credibility and visibility—because now you are on the Island of Individuality. After all, how often do you meet someone who has written a book?

This is how you create a WOW! You WOW your way into people's minds. Their awareness and their perception of you are transformed in that instant when you give them your book.

You don't sell your book. Your book sells you.

It is not what you think about yourself that matters; it is what your prospective clients think about you that matter.

Your brand is more than just a name, a logo, colours, a slogan, or a tagline. It is an identity that comprises all of these as well as the consumer's awareness or perception of your brand.

The first question that a potential customer asks is, "Have I heard about it or seen it before?" This is awareness. If your brand has better visibility, it also has greater brand awareness in the marketplace. Visibility is gained through advertising and sending out positive and powerful marketing messages.

The second question is, "Can I trust this brand? Is this a quality brand?" This is credibility. If you can establish your brand's popularity through association, acknowledgement, or achievement, then it gains credibility. However, if your brand also has a book written about it, it has much more to offer. It is a brand that has the power to transform.

Think Apple. Think Starbucks. Think Virgin Airlines.

Just look up books about any of these brands and you will find at least a dozen of them on Amazon. Whether it is a biography of Steve Jobs, a book written by Howard Schultz or Richard Branson, or books about different aspects of the brand—you will find plenty of reading material.

Why? These brands are worth writing about.

Are you worth writing about as an individual? Unless you are famous or have done something extraordinary, no one will write about you; but that does not mean you cannot write a book on your own.

It does not have to be a memoir or an autobiography. In fact, it should not be. Very few people are likely to be interested in reading your memoirs unless you are famous or notorious. However, you can still write a non-fiction book that will make people sit up and take notice of you as a person and as an author.

You know more than your reader about *something*. It could be related to your profession, or it could be a series of insights or experiential wisdom that you have gained. It will transform you from being perceived as someone who is ordinary, to someone who is an authority.

The Ladder of Wealth

There is a method for attracting opportunities to create wealth. It involves you understanding the process of going from someone who is unknown and in the basket of boring, to someone who confidently stands out and gets recognised as an authority on order to create wealth. This process follows the steps on the Ladder of Wealth.

There are four steps on the Ladder of Wealth:

1. Unknown
2. Known
3. Respect
4. Wealth

If you want to go from being unknown, from being just another individual in the basket of boring, to someone who is substantial and trustworthy—it can be a long journey. That is, if you fail to understand the key to Branding by WOW.

Branding by Authoring is the most underutilised and, at the same time, the most easily achievable method of creating a WOW and establishing your own Island of Individuality.

Sure, writing a book is not easy. But nor is it impossible. This book will show you that it is possible to write a book in no time. It took me less than a year to write my first book, less than 10 hours to write my second book, and approximately three hours to write this book.

There is a systematic method to writing a book. If you follow this method, it is possible to write a book in as little as three days.

Now, if you had three days to work 'on' your business, what would you do?

That is right—write your own book. No more procrastination. No more doubts. Create a complete transformation with your own book. Not just a transformation in how people perceive you, but also a transformation in someone's life every time they read your book. When you write a book, people perceive you as the authority on that subject.

When you write your book, you go from the bottom step of the Ladder of Wealth—unknown—straight to the top—wealth. Why? Your book makes you well known and respected, all at once.

Whatever you do, be different—that was the advice my mother gave me, and I can't think of better advice for an entrepreneur. If you're different, you will stand out.
—Anita Roddick

To find out more about branding, visit
www.MasterYourWow.com .

Reflective Questions

What was the most valuable message you received in this chapter?

_____

_____

_____

What will you do different based on what you've learned?

_____

_____

_____

How will you ensure you do what you've written above in the previous question?

_____

_____

_____

What's been your WOW moment whilst reading so far?

_____

_____

_____

Notes

CHAPTER 2

Transactional vs. Transformational

Transactional vs. Transformational

If you are not willing to risk the usual, you will have to settle for the ordinary.

—Jim Rohn

Every day you interact with people. At work, you interact with colleagues, business partners, or customers, and in your personal relationships, you interact with family members or friends.

Do you imagine yourself ever making a difference in their lives? Or do you just treat every interaction as a routine everyday affair?

You transact or exchange information when you interact with someone.

Every interaction is an action. Most of your actions are intended to fulfil a need. For instance, you go grocery shopping because you need to eat, drink, brush your teeth, and do your laundry.

Therefore, you may go to a shop and buy things such as fruit, vegetables, meat, water, juice, a toothbrush, toothpaste, dental floss, detergent, and so on.

What are you doing?

You are merely going through the motions required to live or exist. You are not doing anything out of the ordinary. You are just doing what everyone else does. You are just doing what is expected of you.

This is doing the Transactional.

You exchange your time, effort, and money for material or products that you need in order to live.

It does not create any waves. It is not hard to do. It is normal. It is ordinary.

You may even say it's boring, but it's necessary. It is something you have to do every day. You have to sleep then get up, eat, drink, brush your teeth, go to work, play, meet people, and at the end of the day, go back to bed.

You have to do this day in and day out. There is no way you can avoid doing most of it.

It's routine.

Nobody expects you to climb a mountain or swim across the English Channel. However, if you do the unexpected, then you are doing something out of the ordinary.

You are doing something Transformational.

You are making a splash. You are creating waves. You are getting other people's attention.

This is what gives you the potential to raise yourself from living an ordinary life like most people do. The potential exists in all of us. What you do with this potential is what separates the extraordinary from the ordinary.

You can rewrite your CV many times; but no matter how many times you rewrite it, you are still doing something ordinary. However, if you wrote a book and sent it along with your CV, then isn't that extraordinary?

Imagine how it can transform your potential future employer's perception of you.

This is transformational.

You need to do the transactional because it's necessary. It's inevitable. But when it comes to doing something transformational, it is optional. You choose how your life will be.

Will it be ordinary? Or will it be extraordinary?

You cannot avoid the transactional. You have to do it because it is required. However, in the process, we tend to ignore the transformational and lose sight of what is really possible.

Do you need to do something transformational? That's a question the answer to which only you can provide.

You cannot afford *not* to do the transformational if you want to be healthy, wealthy, and successful. By being transformational, you attract better people in your life, attract better and more clients to your business, attract more opportunities, create more wealth, and have the opportunity to transform not just yourself and your own life, but also the lives of the people around you.

By doing the transformational, you have the opportunity to transform the world around you. You can make it a better place. You make a positive impact and leave a lasting impression.

You Don't Sell Yourself by Saying, "I Am an Ordinary Person."

When someone asks you what it is that you do for a living, you generally tend to say that you are 'an' accountant, 'a' designer, 'an' executive, 'a' doctor, 'a' mechanic, 'a' manager, or even 'a' CEO.

That is, you say that you are just one among a million other accountants, designers, executives, doctors, mechanics, managers, and CEOs. You are just another drop in the ocean, another grain of sand on the beach, or just another ordinary person.

But you are an individual. So demonstrate your individuality when you tell others who you are.

You could be 'the' accountant who helps his or her clients save money.

You could be 'the' designer who creates attractive artwork to get your clients noticed.

You could be the executive who gets things done in the most efficient and pleasant manner.

You could be the doctor who enables a quick recovery through holistic treatment.

You could be the mechanic who guarantees better performance when he or she repairs something.

You could be the manager who improves productivity in people to grow profits.

You could be the CEO who's multiplied his or her company's revenues.

You must *create* the role you play. If you do not create your own character, you will be a nameless, faceless, and perhaps even voiceless extra in your own life.

You can't play a supporting role in your own life, can you? No. You are reading this book because you want to define your own personality with a clear vision and conviction of what it is that you can do that others cannot. You want to differentiate yourself from others.

When you go to a supermarket, you choose brands that appeal to you. In spite of the fact that there are a dozen or more choices, you choose a particular brand. Why? That's because this particular brand is well known and respected among the other "me-too" brands.

So don't say, "me too." Don't say, "I am 'a' someone" or "I am ordinary." Say, "I am 'the' person who makes a difference to people's lives, because I do the extraordinary.'"

You'll never get anywhere by saying you're the same as everyone else. You have to stand out—and to stand out, you need to be known and respected by offering the promise to deliver something out of the ordinary.

You don't sell yourself by being ordinary. When people see you as someone extraordinary, they will be interested in you.

You suddenly become known; you engage their attention, and thereby you have the opportunity to gain their trust and establish respect.

Transactional exchanges are a part of your life. You cannot avoid mundane tasks, but you should not let your energy get bogged down by doing them. You should find the time and the strength to do the extraordinary. In fact, learn to delegate the tasks you're not good at or don't have the time for and focus on the highest return on investment for *your* time. This will mean that you will have more time to do the things you love in both your professional and personal life.

That's when you'll make people sit up and take notice of you. You can even make a difference in other people's lives; but in order to do so, you need to first make a difference in your own life. You need to see yourself as someone who is special.

If you don't see the spark in your own self, how can you illuminate your presence when you step on the stage?

See Yourself Through the Eyes of Other People

Do you see the difference between yourself and the rest of the people around you? Do you see the potential to do something extraordinary and transformational?

If you consider yourself as someone ordinary, do you think others will treat you any differently?

It's raining outside, and you are in your office or at home. Imagine you're on the third or fourth floor. You open the window and look outside. What do you see?

Countless umbrellas are bobbing up and down the sidewalk.

They are all nondescript. They all look the same. You can't tell one from another, can you? One of them could be you. So how do you differentiate yourself?

You can wear a unique suit every time you're in the public eye, you can carry an umbrella which is a unique colour, you can use the same colour theme, you can give a consistent and captivating presentation—whatever it is, you should ensure you are consistent at standing out and getting noticed.

An optical phenomenon makes a rainbow appear in the sky. But are they real or an illusion?

Rainbows are real if you realise that white light, or light as we ordinarily see it, consists of seven colours that are merged. Rainbows are unreal if you don't know or don't believe in the individuality of each colour.

You can carry a uniquely coloured umbrella, but will other people believe the optical phenomenon?

Are you trying to create an illusion because you don't really believe in your uniqueness? A superficial attempt to create a personality that doesn't fit you will not fool others.

If you think you are not a champion, you cannot credibly carry that umbrella.

You have to know and believe in your heart that you are a champion.

Stop looking at yourself as others see you and start looking at yourself as you would like to be seen by others. Unique, not ordinary.

Only when you change your own perception of yourself can you expect others to change how they see you.

Unleash Your Gifts

In order to understand how you can use innovation to change people's perceptions, let's look at some popular brands that changed the way consumers behave or experience something that was ordinary into something extraordinary.

In the world of personal computers, Apple chose to be different. You either buy a PC or a Mac. The PC is nondescript, even though you have many brands to choose from. Apple innovatively transformed all the elements to make it a unique experience, from the design and hardware to the operating system and software applications.

Apple similarly transformed the way people consume music. You either bought an MP3 player or you bought an iPod. Nobody refers to a Macintosh as a PC or a MacBook as a notebook or laptop. Similarly, you don't refer to an iPod as an MP3 player.

You also don't call an iPad a tablet.

'The' MacBook, 'the' iPod, and 'the' iPad are examples of the transformational. They changed the way people use 'a' PC, 'an' MP3 player, or 'a' tablet.

Similarly, you can either go to a generic café to get a coffee, or you can go to Starbucks.

It's not just your professional impact that you transform by doing the transformational. It's your life.

You go from being someone who is good at his or her job to someone who is exceptional. You go from being an ordinary son or daughter to being someone who is held up as an example by other parents.

You go from being unknown to being widely known. You go from being ignored to being sought after.

If you want to lead an extraordinary life, find out what the ordinary do—and don't do it.

—Tommy Newberry

To learn how to consistently make a transformational impact, visit www.MasterYourWow.com.

Reflective Questions

What was the most valuable message you received in this chapter?

_____

_____

_____

What will you do different based on what you've learned?

_____

_____

_____

How will you ensure you do what you've written above in the previous question?

_____

_____

_____

What's been your WOW moment whilst reading so far?

_____

_____

_____

Notes

_____

_____

_____

_____

_____

_____

_____

_____

_____

_____

_____

_____

_____

_____

_____

_____

_____

_____

CHAPTER 3

Understand the Ability to Impress

Understand the Ability
to Impress

Whatever the mind can conceive and believe, the mind can achieve.

—Napoleon Hill

When you say, "WOW!"—what do you mean? You are impressed with something that someone else has done and you express your admiration by saying, "WOW!"

You say it when you are excited about doing something because it is not any mundane or everyday thing. It is something that is not ordinary or boring. It is something that makes you feel good.

You say it when you are enjoying yourself. You are having a wonderful experience. It's aroused all your senses, and you want to make the most of this feeling.

It's what the climber feels when he reaches the mountain summit. It's what the runner feels when he reaches the finish line. It's what you feel when you take a sip of cool lemonade on a hot day.

It's the sense of elation that you get from doing something that you've never done before. It's an expression of joy when you find a spot in a crowded parking lot. It's a sense of belonging you feel when you exchange hugs with family members you are seeing after a long time.

In other words, it involves success, joy, passion, motivation, confidence, ecstasy, love, gratitude, and many such positive emotions.

It is an emotional state.

The State of WOW is a state of mind.

It is a state in which you are consistently motivated to do the unexpected.

It could be the state of motivation that helps you generate a great idea for a seminar or workshop to enable entrepreneurs or businesses to grow.

It could be the state of high energy that makes you deliver a great performance onstage, whether it's a speech, a poetry recital, a dance, or just saying a piece of dialogue with sincerity and conviction.

You can tell from the silence and the sense of time standing still that you are in a State of WOW, and so is your audience.

It could be the high energy that you feel pulsating through your mind and being after you watch an inspiring movie.

It is the moment of revelation when you can see clearly and truly know in your heart who you are, what you are meant to do with your life, and how you are going to do it.

It is often referred to as the moment of clarity, or epiphany, or inspiration.

Now, imagine living your entire life with this sense of motivation, high energy, and inspiration all the time.

This is the State of WOW that differentiates extraordinary

people from the rest. This is what makes a sportsperson consistently deliver winning performances or a salesperson successfully close every sales pitch that he or she makes.

You may say it is motivation or confidence or inspiration, or it's just the way some people have all the luck.

It is not luck. It's a deliberately cultivated state of mind. It's what successful people have that others don't.

It's the State of WOW.

Everyone enters a State of WOW now and then. You feel inspired. You feel motivated. You are in a state of high energy and confidence. You know that you can do anything because you believe you can.

Sometimes it is caused by external stimuli. Sometimes it is due to what is going on within you—your inner thoughts, feelings, and beliefs.

The question is: how can you sustain this energised feeling and sense of confidence at all times? The answer is to stay in the moment and stay focused not just on what's happening outside you, but also on what's happening within you.

Do It NOW

There is an old Chinese saying, "The best time to plant a tree was 20 years ago. Now is too late; but 20 years from now, the best time to plant a tree will be now."

There is no point in having regrets. There is no point in worrying about what will be. Knowing and learning from past experiences and using them to anticipate future outcomes are practical and sensible ways of using your intuition.

The things that you are likely to regret most will be the

things you didn't do, rather than the things that you did. What will be in the future will surely be influenced by what you do now.

The key to cultivating a constant state of enthusiasm and excitement is to be mindful of the moment, your environment, the people you are interacting with, and the emotional and intellectual process that is going on within you.

Carpe Diem. There is no time like the present to do whatever it is that you want to do.

Have you noticed you are always making plans but not putting them into action? Do you put off doing things because you feel you are not yet ready? Do you say you have to practice, prepare, or wait for the right time so that you don't fail?

Of course you are guilty of procrastinating. "Not now, later," you say. Dillydallying and coming up with excuses is just a form of masking your fear.

You have a book within you, and if there ever was a right time to write it, that time is now.

You are afraid of living in the moment. You are afraid of doing something and failing. You are even afraid of doing something and succeeding; because once you succeed, you will have no excuse to fail in the future.

Overcoming obstacles, eliminating excuses, and doing just what you want to do is simply how you cultivate a constant State of WOW.

Success Is an On-going Process

If someone tells you that something has never been done before, your natural instinct should be to attempt to do it.

It is this sense of stepping into the unknown that drove explorers to discover new routes and new lands.

In a way, this is what drives entrepreneurs as well. It's what makes innovation happen. It's what produces transformational results.

Doing anything for the first time is instrumental to success. Doing something for the first time is to experience the State of WOW.

The outcome doesn't matter. It's the experience that counts.

So, you've never climbed a mountain. Does that mean that you can't? How can you know if something is possible or not without even trying?

So what if you've never written a book? So what if no one else in your family's ever written a book? So what if you never even thought of writing a book?

Anything you do is how you do everything.

In other words, you can't do some things well and others not so well. You can't make a half-hearted attempt to get up early, sleep in till 10, and then try to hurry throughout the day attempting to finish your tasks and make up for the time you lost because you didn't make an early start.

You can't write a book if you think you can't.

You can write a book if you think can.

Create WOWs

When you think of great people, what images come to your mind?

Do you picture them crying? Do you picture them as angry, disappointed, or diffident?

Do you see your favourite footballer hesitating to kick the ball? Do you picture your favourite actor having stage fright? Do you picture your favourite comedian in a maudlin mood?

Do you picture Richard Branson cringing with fear when he flies? Most people would consider that blasphemous.

Can you visualise Oprah in a frumpy dress? It would be a crime to even imagine her as anything but elegant, wouldn't it?

Why? It is because they are all in a constant State of WOW. It's something that comes spontaneously to them. The spontaneity is, however, cultivated by years of deliberately doing the best they can.

Have you noticed how when someone yawns, it's infectious and everyone soon follows suit? The person who yawns first is either bored, or he or she had a late night and is tired.

Does that mean that everyone else who follows, who yawns after the first person yawns, is also bored, sleepy, or tired?

No—it's just a behavioural phenomenon. Yawning is contagious. Yawning is, however, not intentional.

When you yawn, you are unconsciously sending out a signal. It's a sign of boredom or fatigue. It's not a sign meant for others; it's a sign meant for you. It's a way of telling you that you are no longer in a State of WOW. It's a sign that tells you to snap out of it before it becomes a habit.

You yawn when you are bored or tired. You are unconsciously transferring your state of mind to others around you.

Similarly, when you are in a State of WOW, you also transmit your sense of wellbeing to those around you. That's how inspirational leaders can transform you to attempt and achieve things you didn't know you were capable of.

When you are in a State of WOW you are extremely enthusiastic, excited, happy, and confident. You are fully charged with energy. This energy is transmitted to those around you.

If you are a salesperson, you cannot sell your product to someone if you are feeling unhappy or if you do not like your customer. You have to enjoy making the sales pitch, and you have to be keenly interested in your customer.

If you are a footballer, you cannot score a goal if you see the goalkeeper as an obstacle looming between the goalposts. You have to see the goal larger and clearer than the goalkeeper and the other players.

When you are in a State of WOW, you convey warmth and enthusiasm. You create WOW all around you. Whether it's colleagues, friends, family, or customers, they will see in you an opportunity to create WOW for themselves as well.

Your state of WOW manifests itself outside you and spreads the feeling among those with whom you interact, creating a transformational change in the environment around you, wherever you go.

It naturally follows that the colleagues, friends, family, or customers will therefore create opportunities for you to succeed. This is how you attract more opportunities, people, and wealth.

"Some cause happiness wherever they go, others whenever they go," said Oscar Wilde. You can either choose to be the one who makes the sun shine wherever you go, or you can choose to be the one who yawns.

The book you write will create a State of WOW even

when you are not physically present. Your book conveys your personality and influences the reader. Your book will transmit your energy and enthusiasm to others when they read it because you have poured your heart and soul and all that you believe into it.

Your book is a battery charged with your energy that others can benefit from. Your book is the magic wand to make miracles happen. Your book is a seed you're sowing now that will enable you to harvest its fruits for the rest of your life.

Can you afford not to write it?

You are what you think. So just think big, believe big, act big, work big, give big, forgive big, laugh big, love big, and live big.

—*Andrew Carnegie*

Discover how to create your own State of WOW.
Visit www.MasterYourWow.com.

Reflective Questions

What was the most valuable message you received in this chapter?

_____

_____

_____

What will you do different based on what you've learned?

_____

_____

_____

How will you ensure you do what you've written above in the previous question?

_____

_____

_____

What's been your WOW moment whilst reading so far?

_____

_____

_____

Notes

_____

_____

_____

_____

_____

_____

_____

_____

_____

_____

_____

_____

_____

_____

_____

_____

_____

_____

CHAPTER 4
The Power of WOW

The Power of WOW

Opportunities don't happen. You create them.
—*Chris Grosser*

What Does WOW Really Mean?

What WOW really means is that you have left an impact on someone, you have impressed someone, and you have had an influence on them that has cultivated positive feelings towards you.

They like you. And because they like you, they now feel closer to you, they feel more attracted to you, they feel some kind of affinity towards you, which means that if you offer them something, if you teach them something, if you ask them to buy or invest in you—they are more inclined and more willing to do that, because you've left a WOW in their mind.

There are so many ways that you can create WOWs, but before I move onto those ways, let me remind you of the most effective tool you can use to give your brand an impact.

When you create a WOW in someone's mind, it means that you have a brand, and the more WOWs you create, the stronger, the brighter, and the more effective your brand becomes. This means that it will be far easier for you to earn money than it was before you created these WOWs.

What you will know from having read my book so far is that the most powerful and effective way of creating a WOW is by writing your own book. When you write your own book in the right way, using the proven strategy that I'm teaching you, you will create several WOWs that will leave such a deep impact in people that you will be remembered forever.

Of course, there are other ways in which you can create WOWs using different methods of branding that I've mentioned previously. However, you can achieve some of the most interesting WOWs by doing the things that people least expect. Whether those things are big, small, or unexpected, they can have an enormous impact on other people's minds and hearts.

When teaching workshops, I have often observed that most people do not notice the smallest things that are right in front of them. Every time I notice these things, I ensure that they are corrected, improved, and enhanced. For example, if I noticed that someone's name was incorrectly written or there was a small error on their name card, I would ensure that was given to my assistant without the individual knowing, and then I would get the assistant to correct that, print out a new name card, and place that name card on the table. The individual probably assumes most of the time that the card isn't there anymore. Once they eventually notice that it *was* there, they may still not notice what has been changed. I then tell them exactly what I noticed and demonstrate that when you can notice these small details, even the finest details, you can use them in a powerful way and improve and enhance them.

You will soon notice that you'll see things that other people do not. Even that small example can create such a big WOW, because it shows you that I am paying attention to each and every detail. It shows that I am paying attention to your needs without you even knowing how important those needs are. This shows how important *you* actually are.

So, the power of creating WOW can have a hugely significant impact on you, your brand, your relationships, and your business.

Impressing Leaves Impression

What do I mean by that? Well, when you really impress someone, it leaves a mark on their heart as well as in their mind. Sometimes you can just leave a mark in someone's mind, and that's great—but if you can learn how to leave a mark in someone's mind *and* on his or her heart, it is far more powerful.

When you really tap into someone's emotion, when you leave a mark in someone's mind and on their heart, it really creates a strong memory within them.

Most people are forgotten. You may well go through your life and only be remembered by a few people, maybe even they will forget about you completely after some time. Even if they don't forget about you completely, maybe they'll only have a vague memory of you here and there.

There is a way for you to create such a strong desire within people that they will never forget you. The way in which you can achieve this is by leaving a strong, lasting impression on them; this creates such a powerful impact that it makes you far more influential.

I love to be remembered, because it's so easy to be forgotten, but to be remembered requires far more effort. Once you know how to do this, however, it is actually very simple. I have already discussed how writing your own book using the right method and presenting yourself in the right way are both very powerful tools, but there are many other factors to consider when you are aiming to make a lasting impression.

Let me tell you about some of these other factors.

Firstly, the way you dress can certainly leave an impact and make an impression. If you consistently dress well, especially when you go to business events, people will remember you for how well you present yourself.

The second aspect is the way in which you communicate. If you communicate very clearly, effectively, and in a very compelling manner, people will remember that. You will also remember that process, and therefore it will become easier for you to create that memory in people, that lasting impression that says exactly who you are. If you are able to communicate very well, it makes it far easier for people to remember you.

The third thing that leaves a powerful impression and lasting impact is your book.

Why is that? Because most people will simply give you their business card and talk to you until you're fed up.

You want to distinguish yourself from the rest.

When you use your book to introduce yourself, you'll forever be remembered as the individual who wrote the book on that subject. When you are remembered in this way, it is far easier for people to refer you and tell other people about you. Everyone gives out their business card, but you gave them a book. You've stepped out of the basket of boring and used your book to shine in the spotlight. You become interesting, and you become more *valuable*. When you become more interesting and valuable, it's far easier for people to remember you, refer you, and recommend you, and this in turn will ultimately allow you to bring in more money.

Your Image Matters More Than You Know

Imagine walking into a business event and encountering several different types of people there. There are some who dress very casually; perhaps they are wearing tracksuit bottoms, a hoodie, and a t-shirt. There are others wearing jeans and a casual shirt. Then there are the people who are dressed in a very esteemed, very smart, very elegant suit.

Now imagine each one were to ask you to part with money for a particular service that you didn't know you had interest in. Without taking communication into account, if they just simply asked you for the money, which one would you be most likely to trust?

I'd be willing to guess that if you did a study with a hundred people, it's almost certain that more people would trust and be more inclined to give their money to the person who's far better dressed in the smart and elegant suit.

The way you dress tells people more about you than they could ever learn through words alone.

What is the individual who has come in a tracksuit bottom and t-shirt immediately saying to you? Does this person really care? Do they take themselves seriously, and are they here to actually make money?

When it comes to the person who is there in a casual dress or jeans and a shirt, it can perhaps give you the impression that they are here for the wrong reasons. They are dressed more formally, but maybe they are just here to pick up a date?

When you notice the third individual, the one who's very well dressed and looks very smart, you say, "Wow! This person takes himself seriously. This person looks after himself. This person values himself. This person has confidence and self-esteem. If I was going to give my money to any of those three people, I would certainly give it to that person. I inherently trust that person to take care of my money. I truly believe they will deliver my product or my service."

Of course, there is always a possibility that they could be a scam artist; however, chances are, if they have written a book, you're going to know you can trust them. You're going to believe in them. You're going to have more confidence in them because they are showing you that they actually take care of themselves, value themselves, and take themselves seriously.

Naturally, there are exceptions to the rule; but in most cases, you will trust the person who's well dressed far more than the one who is not so smart in their appearance. Your professional attire sets out the way you want to present yourself.

Your image matters more than you know, and people are judging you all the time even if you don't realise it. Although the saying goes, "Don't judge a book by its cover," the fact is that you are doing it all the time, even subconsciously.

I therefore suggest you present yourself both physically and through your choice of words in the most powerful way possible. Let me explain the way your image affects you. When you don't dress well, you don't feel good about yourself, you don't feel important, you don't feel valuable, and you don't feel wealthy. But when you dress well and take care of yourself, not only do people implicitly value and trust you but it also helps you trust yourself. It helps you to value yourself, to believe in yourself, it has a positive effect on your self-esteem, and your confidence rises. By dressing well, you are taking care of your image, and this brings more benefits than you could ever believe or imagine.

I highly recommend you start dressing well and taking care of your image, not just for yourself, but also for your clients and your income. You should not underestimate the impact this can have on your success.

Famous Friends

You have probably been told that your network is your net worth. I'm sure you've heard that phrase many times, but it's actually not necessarily true. What really matters is how you *utilize* your network to determine your net worth.

You can have lots of wealthy friends around you, but if you don't utilize and tap into their resources and knowledge or their support, then it won't equate to anything financially. You need to utilize and maximize any opportunity for collaborations, joint ventures, and partnerships with those famous individuals so that you can become wealthier.

Famous people are highly influential; they have large networks, they have clients who spend a lot of money with them, and they have people who look up to them. So, how can you tap into this influence and create collaboration with a famous individual? How do you create a famous friend?

First of all, you have to use your book in a way that will open doors and allow you to connect with famous people. Once you do that, you create a connection that enables you to build a relationship with that famous individual. You will now be able to approach that individual to propose some kind of joint venture or partnership with them. If it is someone who has a large network and influence in that industry and they accept your proposal, you will have the opportunity to get in front of a huge audience. If you know how to monetise your material, your product, your service, then having a large audience will give you the perfect opportunity to make a lot of money. Of course, if you make a lot of money for yourself in this joint venture, it means you're also making a lot of money for your famous friend. It is a win-win situation for everyone.

If you're doing something to benefit your famous friend, they will be happy to work with you over and over and over again. This will mean repeat business for you and larger sums of money coming into your bank account.

You should also consider the credibility and respect that comes with working with someone famous. Just imagine being able to say you are working with someone like this; if you're in the personal development industry, you might be working with the likes of Les Brown, Jack Canfield, Bob Proctor, Marci Shimoff, Lisa Nichols, Marie Diamond, or

Dr John Demartini. This means you'll be working with someone famous and well-regarded within your industry, and when people see you pictured with them, having dinner with them, doing business with them, or running events with them, or if they see you on the same podcast, radio show, or on TV with them, that famous person carries so much power, influence, and credibility that it expands your brand significantly, and your income will just keep rising. These are just some of my friends and colleagues with whom I'm personally connected, and I want to give you the tools to create similar opportunities.

Personally, I am fortunate to have a lot of famous friends in my life. I'm friends with some of the stars of the hit movie *The Secret*, I'm friends with Les Brown, and I'm also friends with some of the top names in the personal development and self help industries. I have even met the likes of Pelé, the greatest footballer of all time, and the famous musician Rita Ora. Not only do I have pictures with all of these people, I also have the contact numbers and email addresses for a lot of them. This means I have access to them, and the most powerful and effective way I am able to do that is by using my book in the right way in order to open those doors and to create connections with famous people and make them my friends.

Your book can do this for you, too.

Know Your WOWs

One of the most beautiful things about creating WOWs is that there are so many benefits. They make you more memorable, impress your clients, make you more influential, and most importantly, your brand becomes more visible and powerful so that you are able to earn more money.

There are some surprisingly easy ways to plan your WOWs—let me explain to you how you can achieve this.

Firstly, you should take some time out of your busy schedule and dedicate this time to getting inspiration from the environment around you. Right now, I'm working on this book in the Caribbean, on an island called Guadeloupe, and I am also teaching my own workshop whilst I am here. At this moment, while working on this chapter, I am right on the ocean and gaining inspiration for new ways in which I can WOW my clients and you, my Reader.

You should allow yourself to be inspired by the atmosphere, to think of things that will leave a lasting impression and impact upon your clients. You can create a list of these ideas as they come to you; they may seem like small things or big things, but all of them will, become important and influential for your brand in the end.

Whenever I am running a workshop, I make sure that I always shake your hand before you walk into the room on day one. Sometimes I also do that on day two and day three, just to make it really personable and to build that connection with you. I also have cards with each individual's names as well as the level at which they enrolled in my WOW Book Camp™ on them. This gives you another WOW moment, because your clients can see that you really pay attention to detail.

Another way I like to grab your attention and create a WOW is by making you laugh; sometimes I even like to shock you, to wake you up and create a WOW by being direct and honest with you.

During my workshops, I will also give away gifts and freebies that you didn't expect to create that WOW moment. I speak to you candidly and tell you about my real life story to be completely transparent. That's a guaranteed WOW because it allows you to relate to me, it makes me more personable, transparent, and authentic, which in turn makes you feel good about yourself, and it makes you feel like you know me better. This creates greater affinity and a WOW impression upon you.

Another way to WOW is by giving out something that people love. I often like to give out chocolate truffles and other sweet treats that will firstly be a small but unexpected gift, and secondly increase your energy and make you feel good. Even small gestures like this create a WOW impact. It doesn't matter how big or small the WOW is; the important thing is that you do something impressive and unexpected that gets your client saying "Wow! That's amazing!"

One other thing I often do at my workshops is show interviews between my famous friends and myself to my delegates. For example, I will show them interviews I have done with Jack Canfield, Loral Langemeier from *The Secret*, and John Demartini. I will show those interviews for absolutely no charge at my workshops, and they are also available on my YouTube channel, my Facebook page, and other social media accounts. This makes you say "WOW," and it also brings in more business for me.

You need to think carefully about the things that you can do to make your client say "WOW!"—the things that will improve your brand, which in turn will grow your income. You can pre-plan these WOWs; however, if you don't want to do this yourself, then you should make sure you hire someone who is experienced and understands the power and influence of WOWs to create them for you. You could even get someone else to implement them if you feel that you can't do it yourself, perhaps if you don't feel inspired or you don't enjoy doing it.

What is most important is to know your WOW in order to improve your brand, grow your income, and have the maximum impact or influence you can possibly have.

Visit my website www.MasterYourWow.com to learn my about the Power of WOW.

If people like you, they'll listen to you, but if they trust you, they'll do business with you.

—*Zig Ziglar*

Reflective Questions

What was the most valuable message you received in this chapter?

_____

_____

_____

What will you do different based on what you've learned?

_____

_____

_____

How will you ensure you do what you've written above in the previous question?

_____

_____

_____

What's been your WOW moment whilst reading so far?

_____

_____

_____

Notes

CHAPTER 5

Master Your Message

Master Your Message

A great brand is a story that's never completely told.
A brand is a metaphorical story that connects with
something very deep—a fundamental appreciation of
mythology. Stories create the emotional context people
need to locate themselves in a larger experience.

—*Scott Bedbury*

The Power of Story in Your Brand

Stories are amazing because they capture your attention so well.

If you look at some of the biggest brands in the world, they all have a story. In fact, if you look at every human being in the world, each one has a unique story, and that story is what determines where you go in your life. It is the same story that is playing over and over in your mind, leading to the actions that you're taking, and determining your destiny, your fate, your future.

In order to capture the power of the story, what I firstly recommend is that you create one for your brand, so that when people hear you speak, they can relate to who you are, and because of the story that you tell, they'll remember you and your brand more vividly.

One of the keys to being a great communicator is telling powerful stories that captivate, compel, inspire, motivate, and encourage people to invest in you, your product, and your service.

If you look back on history you can see that storytelling is one of the most powerful methods of communication. Even if you look back to your childhood—how did your parents used to keep your attention? They would read bedtime stories to you.

What I'm suggesting to you is not only that you use your story to captivate, compel, and engage people, but that you should also monetise that story through the engagement that you're creating and the way you're telling your story—that is essential.

The more you learn and invest in yourself in order to develop your communication skills, to develop your ability to tell stories, and to improve your brand, the more you'll be increasing your income, your client base, and your reach. You'll be having a bigger impact in the world as a whole.

Learn the power of stories—whether it's in your brand, your personal life, or your communication. If you can master the art of telling a story and create an effective system for *telling* this story, you can then apply that skill to any area of your life.

Watch Your Thoughts

If you look into your mind, at every single moment of life you are creating thoughts—*every* moment—whether it's consciously or subconsciously.

What do I mean by consciously, and what do I mean by subconsciously?

By consciously I mean that you are aware of exactly what is happening. So, for example, you can see that there are objects present right in front of you, and you can recognise that with your conscious mind, your conscious eye.

There are also numerous things going on that you're not aware of in this present moment.

Stop and listen for just a moment.

Maybe you can hear the hum of a refrigerator, the sound of cars driving past on the street outside, a bird chirping from a nearby tree. If you listen very carefully, there are many different sounds being generated all around you.

The subconscious absorbs the things that you are not aware of in the present moment but that are still occurring nevertheless.

You must therefore learn to observe your thoughts carefully, creating mental images and consciously moulding them to create the thoughts that you most desire in your life.

The more you create the thoughts that you most desire in your life, the more you will find that they gradually become inseparable from your very feelings. As they become intertwined with your feelings, these thoughts now become your words and your actions. As you become more congruent, consistent, aligned with your thoughts, your feelings, your words, and your actions, you will find that you will start to master yourself and master your message.

The key to life and to achieving mastery and success in anything is nurturing. Just as you would nurture a tree, crops, or flowers from seed to maturity by ensuring they have enough water or are exposed to the correct amount of sunlight, you as a human being require similar attention.

What do I mean by that?

Well, your thoughts are the seed of life, and the more you nurture and take care of your thoughts, the more you plant positive, powerful seeds in your mind. You will find that you will develop and create beautiful characteristics that will aid you and support you in your journey to success and in creating the life that you truly deserve and desire.

Take good care of your thoughts—by doing so, you will create the life that you most want for yourself. As you do so, you'll also be mastering the message that you send out to the world in order for you to live the life that you truly deserve and desire.

Aim for the Heart

As you create your brand, your message, and your story, and you link it to your products and services, you should aim to appeal to the emotions of your client.

If you strike the right emotional chord with your ideal client, you'll find that they will tune in to a different part of themselves. As they feel you caring for them, and as they feel you touching a deeper part of their emotional needs, it will make it far easier for them to make a buying decision. The emotional side of you tends to make instinctive decisions far more easily than if someone tried to sell something to you without appealing to your inner feelings. This is why you'll often see people selling a product or service by tapping into a client's emotions.

It is far easier to sell to someone who feels very connected to who you are, what you value, and what's important to you compared to someone who is just after the money in your wallet. You'll always find that the individual who shows care, nurtures you, and takes some time to be interested in you, is far more likely to be successful compared to the individual who's simply after your money.

I've carefully studied the art of tapping into your mind and using the power of your words, your communication, and your influence in order to master your message. In this way, you will be in tune with your emotions, and you will find yourself connecting with a deeper part of yourself, one that will enable you to feel that the individual speaking to you truly cares about you, and it will consequentially be easier for you to buy into them.

In order to master your message, you have to learn how to get your client emotionally engaged with it, and therefore with your story, your service, and your product. The more people you can engage on an emotional level, the easier it will be for you to get to where you want to be in your life.

Communication Is the Key to Success

You will notice that some of the wealthiest business teachers, some of the greatest orators and professional speakers, some of the greatest leaders in the world, along with some of the greatest salespeople, have mastered the art of communication.

Communication is indeed an art—one that requires two individuals.

The first is the speaker. You as the speaker are the individual who is outflowing, who is communicating outwardly through a combination of your body language, your words, your voice, and the way in which you're expressing yourself.

The second individual is the listener. As the listener, you are the one who is allowing inflow and receiving communication through your words, your actions, your behaviour, your expressions, and your movements.

Both are equally important, because if there is only a speaker and not a listener involved, you will all be speaking over one another and the message will not be clearly received; there will be no crucial balance between inflow and outflow.

Conversely, if there are only listeners involved, the situation can become very silent and wearisome; there must be a balance, there must be one of each, there must be a speaker and there must be a listener.

It is very important when you are communicating with your clients, your prospective employers, or your audience to quickly establish whether they are actively listening to you and to determine whether your message is being received.

So how do you create these listeners?

Well, firstly, you must show interest in them. The more interest you show in them, the more interested they will be. Rather than trying to be interest*ing*, be interest*ed*. You should be enquiring, ask questions, speak but then turn it over to them so that they can outflow and engage in the conversation and you can inflow, listening carefully to their answers. Don't just listen, but *actively* listen; try to see beyond the words that your client is saying. As you start to understand exactly what your client and your audience wants, you will then be able to offer *exactly* what they need. This will doubtlessly make you a far greater communicator, and the results will likely be reflected in an upturn in your income.

It is essential that you take time to master the art of communication through both your speaking and listening skills. Once you develop these skills you will be able to go anywhere in the world and make money, even if you do not speak the same language.

Truly mastering the art of communication requires careful study, and one of the most effective ways to improve your communication skills is to study other great communicators. The more you study great communicators and the more you surround yourself with these individuals, the more likely it is that you will become a great communicator yourself.

One thing that will help you in ultimately becoming a great communicator is that, with practice, you will build up a system of effective communication that becomes natural to you, and communication will then become effortless.

Less is More

Does this surprise you? Doubtlessly, you're used to the opposite.

You think that in providing more, you will get more back. Allow me to challenge your thinking.

Picture this—you're at a business-networking event and you start a conversation with another delegate. You ask them their name and what they do for a living, and they obligingly reply with the information you expected… but they have not quite finished with you yet! Instead of leaving it there, they just go on, and on, and on, and on about some other information, and just when you think they're finished, they go on, and on, and on, and on just a little bit more. You just can't *wait* for them to be quiet! It is very frustrating for you, as you are now on the receiving end of far more information than you ever needed or anticipated.

You will often find that the more you say, the more it turns people off. All that extra information can get confusing, particularly if you're not a very clear communicator.

The fewer words that you can use to communicate your message, the more clearly and powerfully that message will come across. This is far more effective than mumbling a lot of disorganised, incomprehensible sentences that will often only serve to confuse people. When you keep things very simple, direct, and to the point, you'll be sure to keep your client or audience's attention.

The most important thing when you're speaking is that your client or audience is paying full attention to you. When you give someone exactly what he or she wants to hear in the fewest words possible, it builds a sense of curiosity within them. Remember—you only have **nine seconds** to grab someone's attention, and you want to capitalise on this first impression; if you try and cram in five minutes' worth of information, then it's not going to come across very clearly. If, on the other hand, you actually focus on making what you're going to say very compelling and you use as few words as possible, then you *will* grab their attention.

Consider this example—if you said to your client, "Look at that big house over there, it's going to cost you quite a lot of money if you want it. If you don't have that amount of money right now, then you may not get it. If you do have some of the money, however, you can perhaps pay the rest using monthly investments." The client gazes blankly at you, dumbfounded.

Or you could simply say, "I can help you get into a home larger than you thought you could afford."

Compare the two statements and ask yourself: which one sounds more appealing?

Naturally, the second statement is more appealing, because you're saying less but it has far more clout in its simplicity. The previous sentences were far too long and not very clear. Less, for sure, *is* more.

Your Brand Is Not Just a Brand—It's a Service

Through your brand you can serve many people. Now, if you're not used to the concept of service, I suggest you start reading up on the subject right away.

Those who are great in life are service minded—they focus on serving the many—and if you can serve the many, you will certainly find fulfilment, you will find more joy, you will find more happiness, and—more importantly—you will make the money that you deserve to make.

The money that you want is in your prospective clients' wallets; whoever it is that you're communicating with, they are the ones that are putting the money into *your* account. By ensuring that you're serving them well, you will undoubtedly see an increase in your income.

Your brand is also the vehicle you will use to reach out to as many people as you can. This can allow you to serve a lot of people, depending on how you choose to go forward and manage it. You should always remember that it could be very easy for you to become so focused on the money that you forget about serving people and you get selfish. If you truly want to help people, then it's unlikely that you will have issues with money.

If you do not have the income that you feel you truly

deserve and desire in your life right now, then it's down to your belief systems around money. Once you can overcome and *change* those limiting beliefs around money, you will start to see results. You can change them by surrounding yourself with wealthy people, developing wealthy habits, developing the thoughts that wealthy people have, and then you will also start to get the same kind of *results* that wealthy people do. If you're able to implement what they already do or what they already know, you will also benefit from having that same mindset, and you will notice a transformation within yourself.

I want you to know that your brand is your message, your story, but more importantly—it's your way to truly make a difference in the world.

Join me on my website www.MasterYourWow.com to discover more about this chapter, my book, and other additional material to improve your brand.

> *Branding demands commitment; commitment to continual re-invention; striking chords with people to stir their emotions; and commitment to imagination. It is easy to be cynical about such things, much harder to be successful.*
>
> *—Sir Richard Branson*

Reflective Questions

What was the most valuable message you received in this chapter?

_____

_____

_____

What will you do different based on what you've learned?

_____

_____

_____

How will you ensure you do what you've written above in the previous question?

_____

_____

_____

What's been your WOW moment whilst reading so far?

_____

_____

_____

Notes

CHAPTER 6
The 5 Pillars of Wealth

The 5 Pillars of Wealth

Wealth is the ability to fully experience life.
—Henry David Thoreau

What is wealth? It means many things to many people—but what does it mean to you?

Is it lots of money in the bank, or gold and silver stashed in a secret locker or treasure chest? Is it a big house, or many big houses and lots of big cars, TVs, and very small smartphones and tablets?

Or is it the freedom that comes from knowing that you don't have to worry about what you can afford and what you cannot.

Everything comes with a price; wealth is no exception.

If you do not have your own definition and understanding of what wealth means, then—even if you have lots of money—you are still poor in many ways, because you don't know what wealth means to you.

You cannot use someone else's yardstick to measure your wealth. You need to have your own standards to benchmark what it is that differentiates being rich from being poor.

This may come across to you as too philosophical an argument, but wealth is essentially a metaphysical concept rather than a material one.

Wealth on its own is worthless. It's what wealth can do for you, or what you can do with it, that makes it worthwhile or even valuable.

Gold is valuable, but you cannot build bridges or construct heavy machinery with gold. To make machines or to build utilitarian structures, you will need stronger metals like iron and steel, or some sort of alloy that combines the qualities of strength, flexibility, malleability, and resilience to withstand wear and tear. With gold, you can make ornaments and decorations, but you can't build structures. However, you can use the value of gold to buy the right kind of materials required to build bridges or industries.

Gold on its own is worthless. It's the value that is attributed to gold or silver that makes it valuable. This value goes up or down according to political, business, technological, and economic events. The value is, if not arbitrary, at the very least not in your control.

So, like everything else, wealth also comes with a price.

The important thing to remember is that the price you pay for creating wealth should not prevent you from enjoying its benefits.

What Does Wealth Mean to You?

Since I wanted to have a holistic view of wealth, I asked people from different walks of life what wealth meant to them. I also researched philosophers, wealthy and successful businesspeople, scientists and inventors, artists, musicians, and all kinds of leaders and influential people to see what their views were and to understand the true meaning of wealth.

During my research, I came up with five key aspects of wealth that repeatedly resonated with most people. These were Health, Finance, Relationships, Spirituality, and Giving Back.

Of course, the order in which I mention them is not important; I believe each aspect to be of equal importance. And I realised that only by striking a balance between each of these aspects would you be able to have a happy, successful, and fulfilling life.

So, for instance, even if you were able to achieve tremendous financial wealth but in the process neglected your health, then all that money you earned will be of no use to you in the graveyard. Alternatively, if you ignored, antagonised, or repelled the people who truly love you while you were busy with your pursuit of financial wealth, you might end up a sad and lonely person with no one to share the wealth you have created with.

That's why I think it is important to examine all five aspects of Health, Finance, Relationships, Spirituality, and Giving Back in the context of wealth.

The true meaning of how you perceive wealth lies within you.

What wealth means to me need not be what wealth means to you. It's something that you have to explore and find out for yourself through introspection and examining what kind of wealth it is that you want, why it is important to have wealth, and how you are going to be wealthy.

Creating your wealth is a journey of discovery.

However, as with any journey, there are a few general

pointers or direction signboards, which will serve you well in your quest to create wealth.

One important thing to remember is that this book is not just about creating wealth in a transient manner; it is about enabling you to create wealth for life.

That's why I think it is important to enjoy not just the wealth you create but also the process of creating it.

Health: It Is the Source of Your Energy

There is no denying that health is a primary factor in creating wealth and enjoying the benefits of the wealth you create. You need to take care of your health, because it is health that provides you with the energy that you need in order to create wealth.

According to a quote attributed to the Dalai Lama, "Man sacrifices his health in order to make money. Then he sacrifices money in order to recuperate his health." Now, this is not very hard to understand.

You can become so focused on your job or your business that you forget everything else and pour all your energy into creating wealth. What you may not realise is that the source of all your passion and energy is your health.

When it comes to health, there are two areas you need to look at. One is your physical health, and the other—your mental health.

I cannot emphasise enough the importance of maintaining your mental health, because neglecting it can lead to severe psychological complications. It is very easy to overlook a weakening of your mental health, as signs of deterioration in this area are not immediately noticeable. Just as you should take care of your physical health with exercise, you need to keep your mental health active and invigorated through mental exercises.

I personally underwent a lot of anguish and trauma when I lost control of my mental health for about a year and a half. I fell into a deep, dark hole mentally and psychologically because I could not control the negative thoughts in my mind, and I went into severe bouts of anxiety and depression. When you are in such a state of mental stress, confusion reigns, and it is very difficult to differentiate between what is correct and what is not. It becomes a mental prison. If you don't take steps to relieve yourself from stress and consciously direct your thoughts towards positive thinking, it is possible for you to end up in a mental prison without realising it.

It's not easy to admit that you were once crazy, but the fact is that I was. I still am a little bit crazy, but now it is in a good way, because now I know I am in control of my mental faculties and fully aware of what I am thinking. I can now keep track of my emotional and physical reactions.

It is important to nurture and nourish your mental health just like you would your physical health. One of the first things you should start practicing is meditation. Meditation is nothing but spending quality time with your thoughts, allowing them to form and then analysing and interpreting them. However, in order to examine what goes on in your mind, you first need to empty it of all other thoughts, and then allow your thoughts to pass through naturally. You can do this with the aid of many online audio and video tips to meditate, or you can attend a coaching class to learn the basics.

The second thing is to concentrate on your breathing. Find a quiet place, room, or corner and focus on your breathing. This will help you clear your mind of confusion and bring clarity to your thoughts. Paying attention to your breathing is quite similar to meditating, and in some ways, it is a form of meditation.

Another way to nourish your mental faculties is to read. Read something that you enjoy, whether it is autobiographies, biographies, fiction, memoirs, or books on subjects that you are interested in. Another important form of mental exercise that you can perform is to solve puzzles or play games. This could be anything that interests you, such as crosswords or Sudoku, or playing board games like Scrabble or Chess. It has been observed that playing board games stimulates your cognitive abilities of thought and reason.

Sometimes the best thing is to get out of your own head and do something physical in order to distract yourself and get your feel-good chemicals flowing. Even though you may not feel like it, it's often best to do the opposite of what you may think you need to do to in order to actually heal and help yourself.

When it comes to your physical health, you need to consider two important aspects: nutrition and exercise.

I attribute 80% importance to nutrition and 20% to exercise. Nutrition is important because you are what you eat. Instead of following complicated diets, you can apply some simple rules to ensure that you receive ample nutrition to maintain a healthy and energetic lifestyle.

Firstly, eat food that is natural and alive. This means you should consume more fresh fruits and raw vegetables. As much as possible, try to get organically grown fruits and vegetables—these provide safer and more natural sources for most of the nourishment your body needs. Additionally, organic fruits and vegetables will ensure you reduce consumption of any harmful chemicals.

The second rule is to avoid food that will make you fat as this can contribute to low self-esteem and lead to a lethargic lifestyle. How to know what to avoid? Use the BRPP formula. That's 'B(u)RPP' without the 'u', where B stands for Bread, R for Rice, P for Pasta and the second P for Potatoes. This is particularly useful when you are trying to lose weight, and it also enables you to cultivate healthy lifestyle habits in the long term.

As a physical fitness trainer and coach, my advice to you regarding exercise is to focus on activities that you enjoy. This will ensure that you will not only do them regularly but you will also be able to continue doing them throughout your life, thereby bringing you immense benefits in terms of the quality and duration of your life. So whether it is biking, hiking, running, swimming, going to the gym, attending Pilates or Yoga classes; whether it is indoor activities or outdoor activities—you need to discover what appeals to you.

Most importantly, the activity should encourage natural movement of your body, and you should not feel that you are being forced to do it. That's when exercise becomes torture and unbearable. It should firstly be enjoyable to you, and only then will you benefit. Actually, if you do it right, you only need to perform any exercise three times a week for as little as 20 minutes a day. The important thing is to sweat and allow the pores of your skin to flush out the toxins and waste.

Finance: How Small Changes Can Bring Substantial Returns

Finance is about money. It is about earning more money than you spend so that you can create wealth. Why create wealth? So that you can do all the good things that you want to do with the money that you have.

But finance is not just about money. It is also about your attitude towards it.

It's a sad fact that most people think that money or making money is a bad thing. You should realise that money by itself is not a bad thing. It's what you do with your money that counts. If you think that money is not important, then there is no way you will be able to create wealth, because you have put up a mental barrier to creating wealth. You have already decided to be poor.

Consider this important fact: almost 3% of the people in this world control 97% of the wealth. Instead of looking at this as an unfair and disheartening fact of life, you should be able to spot the opportunity in it. The bottom of the pyramid is overcrowded, while there is room and opportunity for you to move up the pyramid.

Why do you work? To earn money in order to put food on the table, provide for yourself and your family, to pay the rent and bills, and in order to survive.

Do you want to just survive, or do you want to live a fulfilling life?

You may publicly acknowledge the need to make money, but deep in your heart, perhaps you think and believe that money is unimportant or even that it is the source of evil. This is a result of many years of conditioning caused by a combination of moral, philosophical, religious, and social discourse and education. You have been told that money is the root of all evil, and therefore you have unconsciously created within you a barrier to creating wealth.

You have been brainwashed, and you need to use your powers of reason to understand why you are not making enough money despite working very hard.

The reason is simple—you are in denial. You either think money is bad and therefore you don't need it, or you think that making more money will turn you into an evil person.

You need to look on the brighter side. If you had more money, think of all the things you could do to make this a better world. Of course, you can always say that you don't need money to do good deeds, but you have to realise that if you have wealth, then you are in a better position to do the things you want to do. Wealth brings you the power and resources to do something transformational instead of the transitional, to do something extraordinary instead of just surviving.

When you work very hard and do not get the rewards you expect, you become stressed and tired. This is when you become confused and unhappy, which leads to a deterioration in your health and relationships; you start to lose control of your life.

What you should do when you find yourself in such a situation is simply take stock. If you are working for someone else and believe that you are not getting paid what you deserve, you simply need to find another job that will pay you what you think you truly deserve. This is important for regaining your self-esteem and self-confidence. However, instead of exchanging one bad job for a slightly better one, have you considered working for yourself? Have you considered becoming an entrepreneur?

Entrepreneurship is nothing if not venturing on a journey into uncharted territories. If you have a roadmap, you will not lose your way. In business terms, your roadmap is your plan or strategy. Do you have one?

According to Brian Tracy, the author of *The 21 Success Secrets of Self-Made Millionaires*, you merely need to put some very simple steps into practice in order to become a millionaire. There are more self-made millionaires than you might have imagined, and every day there is someone who is embarking on this journey. It could be your journey, too.

A few years back, I was in a situation where I was not making much money despite working very hard. Perhaps you are in a similar situation today.

It was then that I stopped and asked myself if I had a technique or strategy to make money. I realised I didn't.

I was on the bottom step of the ladder of wealth. I was unknown. Perhaps that's where you are today.

I realised that in order to create wealth, I needed to climb the next two steps, to become well known and gain more respect. How to do this? By branding myself. What's the best way to brand yourself? As I mentioned before, it's through Branding by WOW.

I wrote my first book—and the rest is, as they say, history. In fact, I am writing my future and creating my life with every word I write, every action I take. You can also brand yourself by learning the technique of Branding by WOW.

Writing your own book could be your ticket to a new life, to being able to afford to do the things that you've always wanted to do.

It is, however, important to do it the right way, and this book will put you on the right track so that you can Master Your WOW, master your wealth, and master your life!

To learn my tried and tested techniques for writing a book, visit www.MasterYourWow.com.

Relationships: Communicate and Co-operate Instead of Controlling

Relationships are important; they define you. Good relationships can provide tremendous impetus on your journey towards success and creating wealth.

Take, for instance, your relationships at work. If you have better relationships with your colleagues, business partners, clients, or customers, then you will have more opportunities to create wealth. Similarly, personal relationships, whether they are with your family members or with friends, can immensely contribute to your emotional and physical wellbeing, thereby energising you to pursue your passion.

The key to good relationships lies entirely within you. Only you have the power to make your relationships work. I have found that there are three simple guidelines that you can follow to create good relationships; these are Communication, Control, and Co-operation.

Communication is the first step to establishing a link between two people in a relationship. Take marriage, for instance. When there is a lack of proper communication between husband and wife, it leads to misunderstandings, creating a widening chasm of mistrust driving potential life partners away. The same is the case with people at work, between a manager and an employee, an entrepreneur and a client, or an executive and a customer.

All of your communication should establish a one-to-one connection, even if you're communicating to the mass market.

The key to this is relating to the person you are communicating with and understanding what it is that he or she expects from you. In order to do this, first you need to listen to what they are saying. Effective communication begins with actively listening to what the other person is trying to convey. So pay careful attention to what they say to you.

Control is overrated.

You cannot control other people. The more you try to, the less you will be able to. The only person you can control is yourself. It is when one person tries to control another person that resistance and resentment start to build.

Once a person decides to resist your efforts to control their actions or behaviour, you might as well be trying to break through a wall. In fact, it's not unlike hitting your head against a wall; the only result will be a perpetual migraine. So stop trying to control others; instead, try to influence them by setting examples or explaining or even demonstrating your point of view.

The more you try to control, the fewer opportunities you will have to influence, and the more you try to influence, the less you will need to control.

Finally, the most productive way to make the most out of your relationships is to be co-operative.

In a relationship between two people, each one of you should have an equal benefit that matches what the other person is getting from the relationship. Put simply, there should be mutual give and take between the two of you.

This is possible only if both of you take steps to understand and help one another.

For instance, consider two people at work. Each has his or her own responsibility. One of them has the responsibility of calling customers, while the other is supposed to write to them. What if each of them does not like what they are supposed to do? Now, it's possible that the person who is supposed to call enjoys writing e-mails, while the person who is supposed to write e-mails prefers to make telephone calls. If they exchanged their responsibilities, they would both be happier, and they would have established a bond of co-operation.

I would also like to share with you a formula that can ensure that your relationships do not fail.

It is D+E=D. What does it stand for?

Dependency + Expectation = Disappointment.

It may appear very simple and hard to believe, but let me demonstrate how it works.

A boy and girl are in a romantic relationship. The boy gives the girl chocolates and flowers every time they meet. After a few occasions, the boy stops bringing chocolates or flowers whenever they meet. The girl is likely to be disappointed. Why? It's because the boy has created a sense of dependency and expectation in the girl to receive flowers and chocolates.

Now, the girl invites the boy over to her place for a home-cooked dinner. The boy is looking forward to it. He expects a great meal and a wonderful ambience. His having a good time is dependent on the girl being able to meet his expectations. When the boy arrives at her place on a Friday evening, the house is in an absolute state, and she has not yet prepared the meal. He is, naturally, disappointed.

Do you see how you can use the formula to avoid disappointment in your relationships? The key is to avoid becoming dependent, not to have unrealistic expectations, and to be prepared for disappointment. This way, you will each be able to stay stable, steady, and grounded in reality.

You have the power to influence your relationships by learning to communicate, relinquishing control over others and having control over your own self, and co-operating with others.

Spirituality: Find Your Life's Meaning and Purpose

Your real worth lies within you. It is waiting to be utilised, and if you don't use it, it will go to waste.

The sad part is: if you are not aware of what's within you, you will never have the opportunity to realise your full potential. In order to nurture your inner potential, you need to stop looking at what's outside and recognise what's inside you.

I'd like to use a metaphor to explain this. Consider a seed. It's small, mostly invisible, and often overlooked. But is it insignificant? I am sure you would agree that it is not. It is this tiny seed that produces a tree.

Yet it is often ignored because we generally only see the easily visible manifestation of the seed. The leaves, the branches, the fruits, the trunk, and even the roots underneath the ground—we acknowledge the presence of the tree, but we do not pay much attention to the seed. We know the seed once existed. We know that the seed was the main cause for bringing the tree into existence. But when we look at the tree, we think the seed no longer exists. Why? We think it is no longer required.

The seed is like your soul. It existed before you were born, but now that you have a form in the shape of a human being, you think that it no longer exists.

You have a body. You have eyes. You have ears. You have a nose. You have hands. You have legs. Do you have a soul?

Do you say, "I am my body?" No—you say, "This is my body."

Similarly, you don't say, "I am my eyes, my ears, my nose, my hands, or my legs." You say, "These are my eyes, these are my ears. This is my nose, these are my hands, and these are my legs."

When you say you are a human being, you are aware of the 'human' aspect. It is what you can see and therefore what you believe exists. It is the visible, tangible part of you.

What you forget about or don't notice is the 'being' aspect in 'human being.'

When you say, "I am . . ."—that's what you are referring to. You are referring to the being within you—your soul. You may call it whatever you want to—soul, spirit, energy, consciousness, god—but you can neither prove nor refute its existence.

The soul, unfortunately, cannot be separated from your body and placed in a test tube to be studied. That's why there will always be a sceptical part within you that will question the existence of the soul. It is inevitable.

However, to deny the existence of your soul is to deny your true purpose. It creates a sense of ennui and prevents you from realising your full potential. So why is it important to find meaning or purpose?

I would like to quote Shakespeare's Hamlet, "There is nothing either good or bad, but thinking makes it so." There is a profound insight in this statement.

If you think something exists, then it does. If you think it doesn't, then it doesn't. So, even if you have all the wealth in the world but are not content, or you do not know what to do with it, then all the wealth you have is of no use, because you are incapable of appreciating it.

On the other hand, if the whole world seems against you, but you believe in your heart that you possess value, then you will realise that value and convert it into wealth.

Steve Forbes said, "The real source of wealth and capital is not material things, it is the human mind, the human spirit, the human imagination, and our faith in the future."

Ponder on these words.

In conclusion, I'd like to narrate a parable and also provide some advice.

There was a princess who had inherited an exquisite necklace of pearls. She was very proud of this valuable possession, and she never missed an opportunity to wear the necklace. It so happened that there was a great ball to which she was invited. The event was hailed to be one of the most important occasions—all the 'who's who' of the time and place would be present.

On the day of the event, as the princess was getting ready for the party, she suddenly realised that her precious pearl necklace was missing. She searched high and low, but she could not find it. She called all her family members and every member of the household to look for it; they could not find it, either. She was depressed and dejected. She decided that she wouldn't go to the party because she didn't have her prized possession.

She was inconsolable, and everyone finally left her alone to cry. At last, when she had finally exhausted the tears of sadness that welled up inside her, she raised her face to wipe away the tears. She looked in the mirror and saw that the thing she was looking for all along was around her neck.

You may not believe in your soul. Or you may have just lost sight of it. Or you may be looking for meaning and purpose in your life. I was in a similar situation, and I found guidance and solace in an organisation called the Brahma Kumaris. It is a spiritual organisation that transcends religious and ethnic beliefs, with people from all walks of life, creeds, religions, professions, nationalities, and beliefs coming together to help each other and make this world a better place.

You can seek guidance from books, spiritually enlightened people, or even organisations like the one I mentioned in order to find meaning and purpose. In the end, it is your journey of discovery to find your inner strength or spirit.

Give Back: Create a Wealth of Difference

Alex Macmillan, who is a very good friend of mine, once told me, "When I give back to the world what I have been fortunate to earn, I always keep this in mind: the best form of giving is to give to those who cannot give back."

Those words struck a chord with me, and I always remember them when I am giving back.

I look at creating wealth as a means to be able to give back to those who are less fortunate. While the saying goes, "What you give, you get," if you truly want to give back, you should not expect anything in return, because you are giving back what you have already received. That's why I call it 'giving back' and not just 'giving.'

This aspect of creating wealth is in a way connected to spirituality and finding your true purpose in life.

You need to ask yourself the following three questions:

Who are you?

Why are you here?

What are you supposed to do?

Now, you have to answer those three questions honestly.

You may not find the answers immediately. In fact, it may take you years to find the right answers, perhaps even decades or a lifetime; but when you find these answers, you will know that they are the right answers.

In order to give something to society, you need to be in a position to do so. If you are constantly engaged in petty jobs trying to make ends meet, you will have no time for giving back. You will neither have time for introspection nor the inclination for finding out your true purpose in life.

It doesn't matter how much or how little you give back; what matters is why you do so. The reasons for doing so should come from within you. It cannot be because it is fashionable or because a religious, moral, ethical, or legal code says you should.

I often travel the world and work with orphan children to give them a vision of hope by conducting sports and leadership camps. During one of my visits to Africa, I heard a heartrending story that changed my outlook on life.

I heard this story from a native woman who lived in one of

the remote villages in Africa and travelled to work in another village through a forest by foot. After a long day of work, when she was passing through the forest returning home, she heard a noise coming from one of the bushes.

She followed the sound and was aghast to discover a fox chewing on a baby's arm. The baby was crying in pain, but it was so exhausted that hardly any sound came out. The brave woman chased away the fox and carried the baby with her.

She had no mobile phone or any of the other modern means of communication we take for granted. Exhausted as she was after a long day's work, she somehow found the strength to carry the baby all the way to the nearest hospital, which was many miles away.

Most of us who live in cities feel proud when we participate in a marathon and complete the 26-mile run. Here was a woman who walked the distance of more than a marathon, at night after a long day's work, and saved a baby's life. And she doesn't even consider what she did as anything exceptional—just what was expected.

This story not only transformed my perspective of life, it also made me realise how fortunate I am. Whatever amount of wealth I create and however much I give back, I know I will never be able to match what this woman did.

It is stories like these that inspire you to go out into the world and make a difference.

When you WOW Your Way To Wealth, remember the journey is never complete. There is always an opportunity to create a difference in the lives of the less privileged around you.

You can only do this if you know who you are, why you are here, and what your purpose in life is.

Create your opportunity to do something extraordinary, something transformational. Give and don't expect anything in return. You can do so only when you know you already have created the wealth you wanted to.

Go forth into the world and create transformational experiences.

> *It's good to have money and the things that money can buy, but it's good, too, to check up once in a while and make sure that you haven't lost the things that money can't buy.*
>
> —George Lorimer

Start your journey of creating Wealth for Life today—visit www.MasterYourWow.com.

Reflective Questions

What was the most valuable message you received in this chapter?

_____

_____

_____

What will you do different based on what you've learned?

_____

_____

_____

How will you ensure you do what you've written above in the previous question?

_____

_____

_____

What's been your WOW moment whilst reading so far?

_____

_____

_____

Notes

CHAPTER 7

Book Your Words to Wealth

Book Your Words to Wealth

If a story is in you, it has to come out.
—William Faulkner

What's the one thing that rich people have been telling you but that you are not listening to?

Write a book.

That's correct. It's not a secret because it's never been kept under wraps; it's a secret because you have not been listening to what every successful person is saying.

Write a book.

When people see you, meet you, or hear about you, what is their reaction?

Are they interested? Or are they bored?

Their reaction is a reflection of how they perceive you.

Which do you want to be? Interesting or boring?

When people know that you are writing a book, or that you have written a book, then you are automatically transformed in their eyes.

You go from being boring to being interesting. You go from being unknown to being unforgettable. You go from just an expert to an authority.

Your Book Is Your Business Card

When you write a book, you are transacting the information in your mind to someone else—the Reader. When you meet and interact with people, you have an opportunity to impart your experience, your wisdom, and your insights. When you have written a book, you are able to do so many times over and in a much more organised manner than you ever could in any other form.

You have the opportunity to inspire millions of minds and hearts. Your life on this planet is important and meaningful. Don't you want to express what your life means to you?

When you write a book, you have the unique opportunity to connect with potentially millions of people who will read it. These connections are much more remarkable and memorable than the connections you make on social networking sites or even when you meet someone in person.

Imagine meeting someone and giving them a copy of your book. How will that person remember you? They will remember you as an author.

Now compare this to handing out a business card. Where does your business card go as soon as you leave the room or the scene? If you are lucky, it ends up with a whole bunch of other business cards in a Rolodex. You are just another 'me-too.' You are just a commodity. You are not a brand. You are not visible. You are not credible. If you are unlucky, though, your card ends up in the bin.

If you give someone a book, they will not only be taken by surprise—because it is not every day that they get to meet someone who has written a book—but they will also look at you in a different way and see you in a different light.

Do you see how anyone's perception of you instantly changes the moment you give them a book?

Your book opens a new world. The recipient reads your book and is then impressed by the wisdom and knowledge that you are sharing with them through the book.

Become an Author—Be Seen as the Authority in Your Field

What will someone who receives your book do with it? He or she will read it immediately. Well, if they are very busy people, then maybe not immediately, but at least at some point when they get the time. Till then, they'll keep it on their desk or on their bookshelf where it is visible. They'll probably even carry your book with them when they go from home to work or back again so they can read it while travelling on the train or waiting for someone at a café.

Do you see the visibility that your book will garner you? Other people will probably ask the reader about your book. Imagine how much more you'll be known and respected? Imagine how that will increase when the reader of your book says, "I met the author of the book."

While they are reading the book, they will think about you, and with every page they turn, their impression about you will change dramatically. You will be transformed into someone who is an authority, who is a giant among ordinary people. You will grow in stature in their minds. You will become credible because you have shared the knowledge and wisdom that is within you with others.

Where does your book put you? It puts you on a stage with spotlights. It puts you on a pedestal. You get noticed because you are interesting.

You go from being unknown to unforgettable.

Your book becomes your marketing tool.

You don't sell your book. Your book sells you.

So whatever it is that you do, whether you are a plumber or a pianist, an engineer or an electrician, a dancer or a designer—you are no longer 'a' plumber, or 'a' pianist, or 'an' engineer, or 'an' electrician, or 'a' dancer, or 'a' designer.

You are 'the' plumber, or 'the' pianist, or 'the' engineer, or 'the' electrician, or 'the' dancer, or 'the' designer who has written a book.

You are not just an expert; you are an authority.

Anyone can claim to be an expert. If you look around you, everyone who claims to be an expert is either broke or trying very hard to make ends meet.

Your book is better than having a giant billboard, because it conveys much more about you and what you do in a more focused and classy manner to the people who matter. There will never be another moment when you will be compared to someone who is ordinary, because you have clearly demonstrated that you are a cut above the rest.

Your Book Is Within You

Did you say you have never written a book? Do you think your friends and family will laugh at you if you tell them you are going to write a book?

Did you say you are not a native English speaker or that it is not your first language?

Did you know that my mother tongue is not English? Did you know that most writers are not native English speakers? No one in my family before me had ever written a book.

Therefore, the day I said, "I am going to write a book", the day I finished writing it, and the day I published it are days when I made history. Of course, there were many who didn't believe me at first, and I had plenty of moments of self-doubt, but all that changed when I showed everyone my book.

I was transformed. And what had transformed me? The book I wrote.

In fact, many times I meet people for the first time and find they already have a copy of my book. That means that they knew about me even before they met me. They tell me that they have read my book or they heard I've written a book from someone else. They tell me how my book helped them transform their lives, lose weight, eat right, live healthy, and be happy.

Is there anything better than that? Knowing that you have influenced and impacted hundreds of lives and impressed hundreds of minds is the best reward and the best return on investment that I've ever received for writing my book.

I've even had the world-famous Jack Canfield, star of the movie *The Secret*, co-creator of the famous book series *Chicken Soup For The Soul*, New York Times Best Selling author, and one of the most sought-after speakers and coaches in the world write the foreword for my book and provide a testimonial for me. As well as this, he's also a friend and a colleague within the personal development industry.

Influential and well-known figures have also received a copy of my book, including the Queen of England and former Prime Minister David Cameron. Both have written letters of acknowledgment, and I have even received a second letter from the Queen expressing her encouragement and appreciation when she heard that I was writing another book.

Now's the time to decide whether you want to spend the rest of your life in obscurity?

Or do you want to be perceived as an authority?

Yes? Then write your book.

How?

That's a good question. You have wisdom. You have knowledge. You have had experiences. You need to share them, but you are so focused on your work, your career, or your business that you need guidance and coaching to write your book.

If you write the right kind of book the right way, then you will be a brand, attracting more people, more opportunities, and more money. But if you write the wrong book, not only will you have wasted time and effort—you can even turn people off and send out the wrong impression.

That's why it is important to know how to write your book the right way. Just as when you go on a journey you need to have a clear roadmap so that you don't lose your way.

That's why I have created a simple package that will enable you to write your book in no time.

All you need to do is visit www.MasterYourWow.com.

On this website I demonstrate, without a doubt, how you can write a book in just 10 hours if you want to. But before you do, I wish to list some of the key obstacles in writing a book, and how to avoid them and overcome challenges.

First of all, choose a subject carefully.

It may sound obvious, but you should write about something that people will find interesting and will want to read. It could be about your profession, your business, or your passion. Don't make it into an autobiography or a memoir; you are not so well known and not yet a brand.

Your objective is to create your brand. Therefore, people are unlikely to be as interested in reading about your experiences as they would be in reading about Richard Branson's, or even mine.

So, while it is not going to be a memoir or an autobiography, it still needs to be written from deep within you. It has to have your own voice but still resonate with your readers. How do you do this? Make your readers a promise that will get them excited to read the book. How do you do this? Say it in the title of your book.

This is just the tip of the iceberg.

7 Problems You Will Face When Writing Your Book

There are a lot of problems you will face when writing your book, but the seven most common problems are given below.

1. The Foreword

    You need someone who is very well known to write a foreword for your book. Why? Otherwise, it's very likely that many people will not read your book, even if you have written a great book. This is because you are currently unknown and therefore not credible. When someone who is Known and Respected writes the foreword for your book, it puts a stamp of approval on it. The problem is, you may end up paying hundreds of thousands of pounds or even millions to someone well known so that they will endorse your book with a foreword. This is a scam. Not only will you be paying for something that is insincere; you are also most likely not going to get any value from that foreword, and therefore all the money you paid for the foreword plus all the effort and time you put into writing the book will go down the drain. How to prevent this? I have a solution for this on my website, www.MasterYourWow.com.

2. The Cover

    You have surely heard the saying, "Do not judge a book by its cover"—but guess what? People judge a book by its cover all the time. That's why you need a professionally designed cover for your book. Otherwise, you might have a great book and all the effort will come to naught if your cover does not attract readers to pick up your book. In fact, a poorly designed book cover can actually repel or turn away a potential reader. Getting a professional cover designed for your book may take you many months and set you back a few thousand pounds. This will delay the publishing of your book and also put a strain on your pocket. How to solve this problem? There's a solution on my website www. MasterYourWow.com.

3. Procrastination

    This is one of the biggest problems writers face. You may have heard of writer's block, but this can only affect you once you've started writing your book. What if you can't even start because you don't know where to begin? This is why you need your own book angel who will help structure your book so that it gets written. It's like building a house—if you don't have a blueprint or a plan, you will not know where to start. How to get your own personal book angel? Find out at www.MasterYourWow.com.

4. Publishing your book

Let's say you have written your book. Now what? Do you know how hard it is to get published? It is very hard if you try to publish it the traditional way. It can be very easy and even a liberating experience if you have a powerful publisher who will support you in your endeavour. Don't let your life's work go to waste because you can't get your book published. Team up with a powerful publisher who will transform your words into a book, and then you can Book Your Words to Wealth. To find out how to publish your book, visit my website www.MasterYourWow.com.

5. Coaching

Just like athletes and sportspeople, no matter how talented, need a coach to motivate and guide them, you also need coaching to write a book. Otherwise, you are likely to flounder in the confusion of your own thoughts and doubts. A coach will help you achieve a sense of purpose, clarity of vision and thought, and guide you through the labyrinthine layers that you need to navigate to see the light at the end of the tunnel. Stay focused and you will enjoy the task of writing. Get a credible coach who understands exactly what a first-time writer, like you, needs. Go to <u>www.MasterYourWow.com</u>.

6. Marketing your book

    When do you start marketing your book? Once you've finished writing it? This is the wrong answer. You should start marketing your book right now, right away. You should start the moment you decide to write it. Why? Developing a website, marketing materials, and channels takes time. You need to get a head start so the momentum you build as you are writing and the 'Wow' you create as you finish writing isn't wasted. This is just one small tip on how to market your book. Learn plenty of other tricks including how to quickly and effectively have a dedicated website for your book up and running in no time at my website <u>www.MasterYourWow.com</u>.

7. PR expenses

    The book that you wrote needs readers. It is just as useful as a doorstopper if it doesn't have an audience. To attract an audience, you need to create some noise. This is called PR, or Public Relations. You will need a grand and glamorous event to launch your book. You will need to invite some well-known people as well as people from the media to this event. How are you going to do this if you don't know anyone? Even this problem can be easily solved. All you need to do is visit my website www.MasterYourWow.com to find out.

There is a book within you.

No matter what you think, there's always been a book within you. It is way past time that you wrote it. Now is your time. This is your opportunity to create history, to influence people, impress them, and impact lives in a better way.

The idea is to write it so that people hear it and it slides through the brain and goes straight to the heart.
                                                    —Maya Angelou

Are you ready to write your book?
Then go to my website now: www.MasterYourWow.com

Reflective Questions

What was the most valuable message you received in this chapter?

_____

_____

_____

What will you do different based on what you've learned?

_____

_____

_____

How will you ensure you do what you've written above in the previous question?

_____

_____

_____

What's been your WOW moment whilst reading so far?

_____

_____

_____

Notes

"Books are the treasured wealth of the world and the fit inheritance of generations and nations."

—Henry David Thoreau

"I worked from 10pm until 1am every night for a year to write the first *Chicken Soup For The Soul* book."

—Jack Canfield

"Broke people have big TVs, wealthy people have big libraries, but the wealthiest people have their book in wealthy people's libraries."

—Vishal Morjaria

Write Your Own Book Within Three Days
email admin@WealthForLifeEvent.com
or
visit WowBookCamp.com now!

Printed in Great Britain
by Amazon